AF429998

FASCINATING TEXT MESSAGES

Text To Capture The Heart Of Your Recipients.

By

Jimmy Eminent

INTRODUCTION

There is power in written words. Text message is one of the written words that carry power that influences the reader. You can use text to express your feelings, emotions, sympathy and many more heart felt messages to your readers. A lot of broken relationships has been restored through fascinating text messages, love birds have deepen their loves through text messages, forgiveness, favor has been obtained through it, and much more appreciation have been shown through text messages. It is on the above premise that we have taken time to compile a good number short, brief and fascinating text messages for the use of those who appreciate its value and benefit and those who are still looking for means of doing so.

Many people wish they make use of it but lack the gimmick behind constructing it to be brief, short and specific and also carry the in-depth meaning to the intending the recipients.

However, some words that are commonly used in it's short form while writing text messages (SMS) would be found here e.g u,ur,urs etc.These words are well understood in SMS world and are simply covered just like some grammatical expressions are covered by poetic license in literary works.

To make the book simple and easy to understand,it has been divided into different parts according to the headings and sub headings.

I assure you that you will find it interesting.

Thanks.

Jimmy.

TABLE OF CONTENTS

AFFECTION TEXT MESSAGES

1)   You are a tender Lily in my vineyard, a rosy flower in my vast and a sweet smelling fragrance in my corner. I love u.

2)   To love you is an assignment I must carry out, to cherish you is a duty I must fulfill. No other thing can take your position in my heart ,I love you.

3)   If loving you is a crime .pathen I am a criminal. If cherishing you is an offence, I am surely an offender, your affection warmed my heart from time to time, I love u.

4)   A vision was revealed to me last night, I was to choose one out of these money, fame and you, I choose you because life is meaningless without u.

5)   Sweet heart u are one in a million, if I come to live in this world a hundred time, I will marry you again and again.

6)   When doctor cannot save my life, balm cannot heal my wound your love possess a healing virtue to do so.

7)   Marrying you is the best decision I have ever made, I don't know what would have become my lot if I had not taken the decision.

8)   Loving u is like battle started like child play, but difficult to put out like harmattan fire, I love u.

9)   Out of sight is not of mind,you are always in my mind, I love you in a million times.

10)   U must be a thief bcos u stole my heart, u must be fire wood u keep burning in my heart too much. Sincerely u are too much.

11) Dreaming of u is exciting, staying with you is sweet, having you around is wonderful, my mind is on you.

12) You are a rose of Sharon, the lily of the valleys,as the lily among thorns are you among woman/man, you mean a lot to me.

13) In a cold morning, your love keeps me warm like a burning coals, in the heat of the day, it is alike a cold water that cool my thirst one love keep us together.

MISS YOU

1.   Out of sight is not out, mind you are always on mind. I miss you

2.   It is when you left that I realized two people of like mind compliment each other. I miss u.

3.   It has not been a easy task eating, sleeping and doing things alone, I miss you.

4.   Infact missing you is an understatement I am seriously hungry of your warma cuddling, indeed I miss u.

5.   In most time loneliness kill faster than poison please come back quickly, I am missing u.

6.   You have left me at the mercy of midnight cold since no one can substitute your place, I miss you.

7.   I know sometime, someday we shall see again, I miss you.

8.   Life is rarely interesting whenever I cannot find you around me, your love, care and encouragement are like pouring cold water on hot surface, I miss you.'

9.   We are equally born but not equally talented.   Since we departed, I always remember the talent with which you cheer people up during challenges, I miss you.

10. It has been seven month, three weeks, twelve days, fifteen hours, forty minutes and twenty seconds, since you left, I keep on counting when you will be back. I miss you.

11. The word hello means

H – How are you?

E – Everything is okay

L – like to hear from you

L – love to see you soon

O – obviously

I miss you

12.   The pain is not on the day we miss dear ones, the pain is really when you live without them and ur mind really want them. I miss you.

13.   Candle may stop melting ,
Wind may stop blowing ,
Bird may stop flying ,
Heart may stop breathing
Fishes may stop swimming
But I will never stop missing you

14.   R is for Red

Red is for blood

Blood is for heart

Heart is for love

You is me

Me is you

I miss you.

WOOING TEXT MESSAGES

1)   No words of text can describe the extent of your love in my heart you are such a lady that I desire

2)   The first time I met you I knew I met a rarity of beauties and epitome of humility. I want you to be mine.

3)   I am in short of word to express the reasons for loving you so natural. Indeed I love you.

4) Your   thought   has   completely overwhelmed my hearth since we talked. Tell

me the secret of what I need to win in you. You are such a lady of my dream.

5)   As the apple tree among the trees of forest, so you are among the peers

6)   Much water cannot quench your love in my heart neither can the flood drown it. If I give all my substance for the sake of your love, it worth it.

7)   Beauty and humility are two things you can rarely find in a single lady, it is usually either of the two but I found both in you. I admire you.

8)   The price of a virtuous woman is far above rubies, keep it up. You mean a lot to me.

9)   You are a jewel of inestimable value, I hold you in a high esteem.

10) There are many fishes in the ocean, but the golden one is the best, among which you are.

FRIENDSHIP TEXT MESSAGE

1.   Our friendship is the best to be described as God ordained.   God has chosen us to be friend and so we shall be for life.

2.   It is a wise saying to say a friend in need is a friend indeed. I am happy to have you as my friend.

3.   Life is interesting only if you spend it with right people. Truly you deserved to be called a friend.

4.   Friendship is a single soul living in two bodies, you are such a wonderful friend.

5.   One of the yardsticks to measure true riches is quality friends and people a man has around, I am rich because I have you as a friend.

6.   You indeed have touched my life in a way you may not notice, you have imparted value into my life in a way that you have not perceived. Your friendship is a blessing to me.

7.   I thought of the richest man that ever lived, I remembered Solomon, I thought of a great leader, I remember Joshua, I thought of great evangelist, I remember Paul, when I thought of a reliable friend, I remember you.

8.   Having you as a friend is like possessing a precious jasper stone, you worth to me more than a million.

9. Gold should be sold to those that knows it's value, you are a jewel of inestimable value, I hold you in a high esteem.

10. Good friends are hard to find, harder to leave and impossible to forget.

BEST WISHES

a. Marriage
b. Examination
c. Health
d. Birthday

MARRIAGE WISHES

1. I wish you happy married life and a home like heaven on earth.

2. Happiness as light as air, love as deep as ocean, friends as solid as diamonds and success as bright as gold, this are my wishes for you.

EXAMINATION

1. Reward of hardworking may not come immediately but in good time it shall appear, best of luck.

2. As u prepare for your forthcoming examination, may God crown your effort with success and may u come out in flying colours.

3. I always intercede before God for your success, go and write your exams and excel.

4. You will not only succeed in your exam but in all endeavours of your life. Success galore.

5. May God help you during your exam and bless you with great marks.

6. Remain calm, study with passion, step into the exam with courage success is sure.

7. The Lord shall grant you a studious mind, retentive memory and solomonic wisdom, best of luck.

8. Flying in the aeroplane of ambition and land in the airport of success good luck.

GOOD HEALTH WISHES

1.   None of the diseases of the wicked will be your portion, I am the Lord that heals you, thus saith the Lord.

2.   I learnt u are not feeling well, so I brought you flowers to make you feel happier and healthier, it is well with you.

3.   The balm of gilead, will relieve you of your pain and the joy of the Lord will be your strength.

4.   I hope you are getting better, your absence has a created a vacuum, this is why I say get well soon.

5.   I wish you speedy recovery as you mean a lot to me as well as your health I plead sound health to ur bone and marrow.

6.   The healing virtue of the Lord will flow through you from head to toe and it will make you whole.

BIRTHDAYS WISHES

1.   Not just a year old but a year better, happy birthday.

2.I wish you long life, sound health and many more prosperous years.

3,Your birthday shall convert all hatred to love, all failure to success, all punishments into blessings and all challenges to opportunities happy birthday.

As you celebrate a special day of your life, may it bring your way all good things that future holds for you.

2.   Concluding another year in your life will usher you into another, fruitfulness.   Happy birthday, round of success, another batch of greatness.

3.   As another year is added 2 your year 2day. You have increased in age, may you also increase   in   wisdom   in   knowledge, understanding   and   prosperity.   Happy birthday.

4.   Yours soul is pure your heart is priceless, may you live to fulfil your destiny happy birthday.

5.   From a lovely friend for a lovely reason. Lovely time from a lovely   way I say have a lovely birthday.

6.   **This new age of yours shall usher you into unprecedented   progress and remarkable achievements.**

7.   **As you add another year to your years you shall move from grace to GRACE, strength to STRENGHT, little to ABUNDANCE bright like sunlight and shine   like firmament of the morning, congratulations.**

APPRECIATION TEXT MESSAGE

1.   If good deeds cannot be adequately repaid, it should be graciously appreciated. Thank u.

2.   U hv given ds measure of cup for d sake of God. He promised to repay, he will surely repay u in million folds, he will multiply you for abundance and promote you for greatness. Thank you.

3.   No word is adequate to express ur kindness to me. God that reward every work will surely reward you.

4.   My success story is not complete w/out u, I will ever live to acknowledge it. Thank you so much.

5.   A friend in need is a friend indeed, that is you. Thank for being there for me all the time.

6.   Your hands of fellowship during my time of scarceness is like a precious ointment on a dry skin. May God bless you the more.

7.   You can give without love but you cannot love without giving. Thanks for your love that prompt your giving.

8.   Love and care are two inseparable things. Thanks for being caring.

DISAPPOINTMENT TEXT MESSAGE

1.   With the level of trust I repose in you, I never expect you could do this to me. I am disappointed in you.
2.   My expectation from you is higher than what you exhibit yesterday, you disappointed me.
3.   I count so much on you but u let me down. It is rather unfortunate.
4.   Human being will always be human, if ten people predicted to me about your misbehavior I still will not believe. Infact you disappointed me.
5.   It is a true saying the human confidence is vanity. I am disappointed.

6.   It takes a couple of second to say hello, but forever to say goodbye.

7.   You are the one who have given me my own share of bitter experience in relationship, but remember that whatever a man sow he shall reap.

8.   I never knew that loving someone is an offence until you prove it to me. U are indeed a bitter experience to my life.

9.   I have realized too late ago that you are deceiving me all this while, u have made true love a mirage for me. However, I deserve it by giving my love to an unfaithful entity like u.

10.   Oh, you strip out tears from my eyes to roll down my cheeks uncontrollably. Only God knows how you have broken my heart. How I wish I have been more careful.

11.   What is happening now is like a fire in my bassoon, but do I really deserve this?

CONGRATULATORY TEXT MESSAGE

1.   I heartily felicitate with you on your new position may you continue to rise and never fall. Congratulations.

2.   It is a true saying that whatever a man sow he shall reap, your commitment and hard work, with the grace of God has singled you out for   this enviable position.   Ride on, congratulations.

3.   Congratulations on your promotion from the company of single to married.   Happy married life.

4.   U're ordained to excel, designed to shine and predestined to be great. Congratulations.

5.   Acquiring new thing is tantamount to finding the favour of God. More of such good things, congratulations.

6.   To get to the top is hard, to remain on the top is harder, may u find more of God's grace and power to continue   to remain   on top. Congratulations.

7.   I heard your success story and I was excited. I rejoice with you ,Qmore power to your elbow. Congratulations.

RECONCILIATION TEXT MESSAGE

1.   *Not minding that u have hurt my feelings, I have made up mind to forgive u. u are pardoned.*
2.   *Can two walk except they agree, let us agree and move on.*
3.   *Let us stop loving like cat and rat for it will do us no good. We should let go our difference and allow life to continue.*
4.   *No rancor or rift will erode d memory of d pleasant time we have spent together, I am always ready to embrace you again. We shall be friend forever.*
5.   *How good and how pleasant it is for people to dwell together in unity, life is mostly interesting in an atmosphere of peace and unity. I still love you.*
6.   *Since there is not yet alternative to loving you, there is nothing to do than to accept you back into my life.*

7.	I urge you to let us settle our dispute once and for all in order to move to the next realm of our friendship.

8.	Since you have realized your flaws I have no option than to forgive you but I only demand one thing from you. Turn over a new leaf.

JOURNEY MERCY TEX MESSAGES

1.	The Mark of God's divine protection shall be engraved on you, you shall go and come back in peace. Safe journey.

2.	May the light of God surround you may his love encompass you may his power protect you. May his eyes watch over you, safe journey.

3.	We depart in peace, we shall also meet in peace, safe journey.

4.	As birds fly in the air without hitch so shall you travel in the balloon without crashing, safe trip.

5.	No matter the channel you take for your journey sea, air, water ,rail or road the sure protection of God shall abide with you. Amen.

6.	As you depart to your new destination this morning, I wish you a stress free trip, safe journey.

7.	The Lord shall preserve your going out and your coming in according to his promise. Go well.

SYMPATHY AND CONDOLENCE TEXT MESSAGES

1. For Zion said the Lord had forsaken me, can a woman forget her sucking child and not have compassion on son of her womb, even if they forget yet. He said he will not forget you.

2. May the love of God help you through in all your days as you bear the pains of this bereavement

3. I was shocked to receive the news of your father's / mother's departure, may God grant you the fortitude to bear the irreparable loss.

4. I felt sad to hear the news of the accident may God grant you quick quick recovery.

5. The journey of life is saddled with one challenge or the other and at one time or the other, my brother summon courage tough time never last but tough people do.

6. Death is an inevitable price that every living must pay, may God fill the vacuum he /she has created. Take heart

7.   The downfall of man is never the end of life.   I see victory   ahead of   you in this challenges. It will soon be over.

8.   At the end of a thick of darkness of night is the brightness of the day. There is light at the end of tunnel. It shall soon turn to you for a testimony.

WARNING TEXT MESSAGES

1.   Watch your thought, they become your words,
Watch yours words they become your habits
Watch your habit they becomes your character
Watch your character it becomes your destiny .

2.   *If you don't stand for something, you will fall for anything.   Try to always stand for something good.*

3.   *Whatever you can accomplish in the morning don't differ it till the afternoon.Delay is dangerous*

4.   *Evil association corrupt good manner*

5.   *Treat others exactly the way you want them to treat you.*

6.   *Little patience in the moment of anger can save you in a thousands of trouble.*

APOLOGY TEXT MESSAGES

1.   To err is human to forgives is divine, kindly pardon.

2.   I knew I hurt your feelings, please forgive and forget.

3.   I later realize I have done foolishly, please accept my sincere apology, I promise it won't repeat itself.

4.   I had like to apologise because of the value I place on our relationship not really because I am wrong. Let us overlook our difference. life goes on.

5.   My action was due to an overwhelmed emotion from the depth of my heart, I say am sorry.

6.   I don't mean to offend you, it was not deliberate. Accept my sincere apology.

7.   Love, relationship and friendship that fail to create room for forgiveness cannot stand the test of time, kindly forgive me so that we can go ahead.

8.   If you are keeping my record of offences, I knew my own page would have been full,

but as I tender my sincere apology, I knew you are kind to delete all my offences.

9.   I will not like to recount the episode of sad event, all I just want to say is that I am sorry.

10.   There is a five letter words, it appease the heart, dissolve   the clogs of bitterness   and heal the wound.   Of offences,   please accept this word from me. SORRY.

PRAYER TEXT MESSAGES

1.   Behold he that keep Israel shall neither sleep nor slumber, he shall keep you in all your ways.

2.   God shall preserve you from all evil, he shall establish you beyond oppression.

3.	The invisible hands of God that rules in affairs of men shall guide you in all your ways.

4.	He that have started good things in your life will perfect it

5.	You will not labour for another man to reap, neither shall you plant for another man to harvest.

6.	The Lord has loaded your spiritual gun with bullets to kill poverty, failure, sickness, and disappointment in you. The next line of action is to go ahead and shoot, please don't miss fire.

NEW YEAR /NEW MONTH WISHES

1.   As you step into this new year/month, you are stepping into success, promotion, riches and sound health.

2.   The invisible hands of the almighty God that rules in the affairs of man will guide you throughout in this new year/month. Happy New Year.

3.   May the breeze of love, joy, and hope blows in your home this Xmas and new year. Happy New Year

4.   I heartily welcome you to another journey of 365 days of abundance joy, good health and promotion. Happy New Year

5.   The angel of God has just published the names of those who will be celebrated for greatness this new year /month. Your name top the list, Happy New Year.

6.   In this new year/month, you shall not labour in vain neither shall you bring forth for trouble, but you shall eat the fruit of your labour. Happy New Year

7.   The Lord will grant all your desire and will fulfil all His promise upon your life.   Happy New Year

8.   It is not the one that is running and the one that is willing but God that shows mercy. In this new year/ month His
mercy shall compass you about.

9.   May the spirit of the season of new year fill your hearth with sincerity and peace. Wishing you Happy New Year

ENCOURAGEMENT, MOTIVATION AND INSPIRATION TEXT MESSAGE

1.   Progress, promotion and outstanding success are not earned on the platter of gold but on dint of hard work, diligence and commitment. Work when you can.

2. *Whatever you find your hands doing, do it with all your zeal because opportunity comes but once.*

3. *You are a divine project, the contractor handling you is almighty God, you shall not be abandoned, you must reach a desire height and become an enviable structure in the city.*

4. *At the tip of every failure is a success, at the end of every darkest hour is the brightness of the day. Keep hope alive.*

5. *Whatever you can accomplish in the morning don't differ it till afternoon.*

6. *As a man perfect his calling so is his ability to function increases.*

7. *Procrastination is the stealer of time, shun procrastination.*

8. *Pessimist sees difficulties in every opportunity while optimist sees opportunity in every difficulty. Be optimistic.*

9. *It is of no use wasting tears upon blotted records of lost years, there are blank pages yet to be filled, you can start afresh.*

10. *Keep your heart with all diligence, out of it comes the issues of life.*

11. *The battle of life to whoever desire victory is no retreat no surrender, fight to finish, watching till victory light shines.*

12.   *Buy the truth, but sell it not.   Stand always for truth.*

13.   *You can never have the second chance of making the first impression, always make your first impression awesome.*

14.   *Wisdom is the principal thing therefore get wisdom in all your pursuit get understanding.*

15.   *The fear of God is the beginning of wisdom and the knowledge of the holy is understanding.*

16.   *If you faint in the day of adversity your strength is small. Be bold and courageous .*

17.   *For though the vision tarries but it is yet of an appointed time. Press on.*

18.   *Be strong and courageous, do not relax until the victory light shines and the camp of your enemy is taken by violent.*

19.   *Greatness in life is not in never falling, but rising each time you fall. You can rise again.*

20.   *The downfalls of man is never the end of his life.*

21.   *The ability of a man to rise any time he fails is what makes him a man.*

22.   *If you faint in the day of adversity your strength is small.*

23. *There is no royal road to success but every road become royal after success.*

24. *Rain of summer, snows of winter, grace of autumn, glory of spring. May beauty of every season give your heart a beautiful reason to smile.*

25. *Love your self first for everything to work for you. You really need to love yourself to go ahead in your life. Best of love.*

26. *Past is a nice place to visit certainly not a good place to stay.*

27. *The tongue has no bone but strong enough to break ear. Bridle your tongue.*

28. *If you really love somebody, you rather show them than to tell them.*

29. *Always do what you are afraid to do in life because to the question of life you are the answer, to the problem of life you are the solution. All are in you.*

30. *You take more risk by fearing to take risk, you anticipate more failure by failing to attempt because of failure. Take a bold step you would not be where you use to be.*

31. *Let your vision be a mission to behold rather than a vision to be told. Think big, start small, act now.*

32. *Don't swallow your option for fear of criticism, in every nonsense there is a sense.*

33.   Stay simple and be happy, when things go wrong, don't get upset, just pray and say I will get through. Always remember God loves you.

34.   What makes a man is not in never falling but his ability to rise each time he falls.

35.   Living in the favourable and unfavourable situation is called part of life, but smiling in all those situation   is called art of life.

<u>*APPENDIX*</u>

U   :   You.

Ur   :   Your.

Urs :   Yours.

W/out :   without .

Bcos : Because.

d   :   the

4   :   for

2   :   to